BOYD COUNTY

DEC 17 2019

PUBLIC LIBRARY

D1716531

INSIDE THE
NFL

BUFFALO
BILLS

BY TONY HUNTER

SportsZone

An Imprint of Abdo Publishing
abdobooks.com

abdobooks.com

Published by Abdo Publishing, a division of ABDO, PO Box 398166, Minneapolis, Minnesota 55439. Copyright © 2020 by Abdo Consulting Group, Inc. International copyrights reserved in all countries. No part of this book may be reproduced in any form without written permission from the publisher. SportsZone™ is a trademark and logo of Abdo Publishing.

Printed in the United States of America, North Mankato, Minnesota
022019
092019

THIS BOOK CONTAINS
RECYCLED MATERIALS

Cover Photo: Adrian Kraus/AP Images
Interior Photos: Rick Stewart/Getty Images Sport/Getty Images, 5; NFL Photos/AP Images, 7, 13, 25, 27; Al Messerschmidt/AP Images, 9; AP Images, 15, 17, 20–21, 23, 30; Ed Kolenovsky/AP Images, 18, 43; Diamond Images/Getty Images, 33; Doug Mills/AP Images, 35; Paul Spinelli/AP Images, 38; David Rosenblum/Icon Sportswire/Getty Images, 41

Editor: Patrick Donnelly
Series Designer: Craig Hinton

Library of Congress Control Number: 2018964767

Publisher's Cataloging-in-Publication Data

Names: Hunter, Tony, author.
Title: Buffalo Bills / by Tony Hunter.
Description: Minneapolis, Minnesota : Abdo Publishing, 2020 | Series: Inside the
    NFL | Includes online resources and index.
Identifiers: ISBN 9781532118395 (lib. bdg.) | ISBN 9781532172571 (ebook)
Subjects: LCSH: Buffalo Bills (Football team)--Juvenile literature. | National
    Football League--Juvenile literature. | Football teams--Juvenile literature. |
    American football--Juvenile literature.
Classification: DDC 796.33264--dc23

TABLE OF
CONTENTS

CHAPTER 1

SUPER CLOSE

The Buffalo Bills got the ball back and with it, one more chance for victory. The New York Giants had maintained possession for more than two-thirds of the game. But the Bills had managed to stay within one point of the Giants in Super Bowl XXV.

It was January 27, 1991. The Bills had a chance of winning in their first Super Bowl appearance, which was in Tampa, Florida. Just over two minutes remained in the game. The Giants led 20–19. Now the game was in the hands of the Bills' star quarterback, Jim Kelly. If the Bills could score, they would likely win.

Buffalo began from its own 10-yard line. Kelly stepped behind the center and began to run the two-minute offense. Teams take that approach when they need to score quickly.

Bills quarterback Jim Kelly celebrates Buffalo's first touchdown in Super Bowl XXV.

STELLAR SEASON

The Bills had a standout 1990 regular season. Their 13–3 record was the best of any team in the American Football Conference (AFC). The Bills' 428 total points were the most in the NFL. That offense was led by quarterback Jim Kelly. He was the highest-rated passer in the league that season. In the two playoff games before the Super Bowl, Kelly completed 36 of 52 passes for 639 yards and five touchdowns.

Kelly and the offense began steadily moving up the field. Behind runs of 22 and 11 yards by running back Thurman Thomas, the Bills moved to New York's 29-yard line in just seven plays.

The Bills had used their final timeout along the way. So on the next play, Kelly spiked the ball to stop the clock. Only eight seconds remained.

Buffalo's fate was on the foot of kicker Scott Norwood. Adding the 10 yards of the end zone and almost eight yards between the center and the holder, Norwood was faced with a 47-yard field goal attempt. A successful kick would give Buffalo the victory.

Norwood could have been a Super Bowl hero. But there was no guarantee that he would make it. From that distance, kickers in the National Football League (NFL) miss roughly as many as they make. Norwood himself hadn't made a field goal longer than 48 yards that year.

Running back Thurman Thomas contributed two big runs to the Bills' final drive in Super Bowl XXV.

The pressure was on. Some players on each sideline knelt in prayer. Others held hands. Some simply looked away.

Buffalo holder Frank Reich received the snap cleanly. He placed the ball on the field. Then Norwood blasted it with his

JIM KELLY

The Bills selected quarterback Jim Kelly in the first round of the 1983 NFL Draft. But Kelly decided that he did not want to play with the struggling team. Instead, he joined the Houston Gamblers of the United States Football League (USFL). He was one of the league's biggest stars until it folded two years later.

With the Gamblers gone, Kelly reported to the Buffalo Bills in 1986. There, he thrived in coach Marv Levy's no-huddle offense. He reached 30,000 career passing yards faster than all but three NFL quarterbacks before him. Kelly benefited by playing with stars such as running back Thurman Thomas and wide receiver Andre Reed. Kelly led the Bills to the playoffs eight times during his 11 seasons with the team.

He was inducted into the Pro Football Hall of Fame in 2002. Kelly remains a popular figure in Buffalo, where the community supported him through a battle with cancer.

right foot. The kicker made solid contact with the ball. After his follow-through, Norwood raised his head to watch.

Millions of people around the United States watched the ball as it sailed through the air. None had a better view than Norwood himself. "By that time," Norwood said, "I knew the kick wasn't good." He was right. The ball had enough distance, but it floated just inches wide of the right goalpost.

✗ Scott Norwood's kick sailed wide right as Buffalo lost to the New York Giants 20–19 in Super Bowl XXV.

MARV LEVY

Marv Levy took over as coach of the Buffalo Bills in 1986. He brought with him a complex, no-huddle offense that helped showcase quarterback Jim Kelly and the team's other talented skill-position players. They went from a losing record to a 10-year stretch in which the Bills had the best record in the AFC. The coach was inducted into the Pro Football Hall of Fame in 2001. In 2006 Levy returned to Buffalo as the acting team general manager. He worked for two seasons trying to help the struggling Bills before retiring again.

Looking back, Norwood believed he did almost everything right on the kick. Almost. "I wanted to hit the ball solid and I did," he said in a postgame interview. "I wanted to get the kick off fast and I wanted to get it high, so it wouldn't be blocked. And I did. I just didn't get my hips into it enough."

Those few inches would come back to haunt Bills fans. The team reached the Super Bowl in each of the next three years but lost all three. Buffalo became the only team in NFL history to lose four straight Super Bowls. As of 2018, Buffalo had never been closer to a Super Bowl victory than those few inches.

The Bills' next-closest call came the following year, after the 1991 season. Washington opened up a 24–0 lead in the Super Bowl. Buffalo put up a fight in the second half, but it was not enough. On a day in which Kelly threw four interceptions, Buffalo lost 37–24.

THE REICH STUFF

As quarterback for the University of Maryland, Frank Reich led one of the biggest comebacks in college football history. Maryland was losing 31–0 to the University of Miami. But Maryland ended up winning 42–40.

Reich had another opportunity for a comeback with the Bills during a playoff game in January 1993. With starter Jim Kelly injured, Reich filled in at quarterback. The Bills trailed the Houston Oilers 35–3 with 13:19 left in the third quarter.

The comeback began when Kenneth Davis scored on a 1-yard rush. Reich then threw three touchdown passes—all before the third quarter was over. Reich added another touchdown pass in the fourth quarter. The score was tied after regulation. Then Bills kicker Steve Christie hit a 32-yard field goal in overtime for the 41–38 victory.

The next two tries were not as close. Quarterback Troy Aikman led the Dallas Cowboys to a 52–17 rout over the Bills in Super Bowl XXVII. The same teams met again the next year at Super Bowl XXVIII. The Bills took a 13–6 lead into halftime. But Dallas roared back behind running back Emmitt Smith's two touchdowns to win 30–13.

Bills fans are still waiting to forget about those few inches.

CHAPTER 2

AFL CHAMPIONS

The American Football League (AFL) awarded six charter franchises in 1959. They were the Dallas Texans, Houston Oilers, New York Titans, Denver Broncos, Los Angeles Chargers, and a team to be based in Minnesota. Before the first game, Minnesota instead accepted an NFL franchise and was replaced in the AFL by the Oakland Raiders. The Buffalo Bills and Boston Patriots were also added that fall. The league would have eight teams for its first season in 1960.

Ralph Wilson Jr. was the owner of the Buffalo Bills. Buster Ramsey was the Bills' first coach. The team began with a 27–3 loss to the New York Titans on September 11, 1960. The Bills had a season-low 113 yards of total offense in the game. The Bills' first win came 12 days later. They went on the road to beat the Patriots 13–0. The Bills forced seven turnovers in the victory.

Jack Kemp looks for a receiver during the Bills' win over the San Diego Chargers in the 1964 AFL Championship Game.

RALPH WILSON JR.

Buffalo Bills founder Ralph Wilson Jr. was the only owner the team had through 2014. He was also one of the men most responsible for merging the AFL and the NFL before the 1970 season. In 1997 the NFL Alumni Association awarded Wilson with the "Order of the Leather Helmet." The honor is given to people who have made "substantial contributions to professional football." Wilson was inducted into the Pro Football Hall of Fame in 2009. After Wilson's death in 2014, Terry and Kim Pegula of Buffalo purchased the Bills for more than $1 billion.

Wilson owned part of the NFL's Detroit Lions before the Bills existed. Then, in 1959 he founded the Bills before the AFL's first season. Few believed the league would succeed, but Wilson played a big role in making sure it did. In 1965 he began talks that led to the AFL-NFL merger. After that, Wilson remained active behind the scenes in league operations.

After four seasons, the Bills still had not won more than half of their games. But that was to change in 1964. The groundwork for the change had begun two seasons earlier. The Bills hired Lou Saban as coach in 1962. After losing their first five games, they finished 7–6–1 that season. Jack Kemp took over as quarterback the next season. The Bills started 0–3–1. After adjusting to the new quarterback, they won seven of their last 10 games.

Bills owner Ralph Wilson Jr., *back row center*, poses with representatives from the other AFL teams in 1959.

Buffalo defeated the New York Jets (formerly the Titans) in back-to-back games at the end of that season. With a 7–6–1 record, the Bills were tied for the East division title. They hosted

WHAT'S IN A NAME?

The Buffalo Bills were named after Buffalo Bill Cody. He was a famous Western frontiersman during the 1800s. In 1946 the Buffalo Bisons joined the All-America Football Conference (AAFC). The team changed its name to the Buffalo Bills in 1947. It kept the name until the AAFC broke up in 1949. When Ralph Wilson Jr. bought an AFL franchise in 1959, he decided to use the former team's name.

the Patriots in a playoff. However, the Bills lost 26–8.

In 1964 Buffalo wasted no time getting hot, winning its first nine games. The highlight of the streak came on October 11 in Houston. Kemp completed 14 of 26 passes for 378 yards and three touchdowns. Receiver Elbert Dubenion caught five passes for 183 yards and a touchdown. Receiver Glenn Bass caught five passes for 147 yards and two touchdowns. The Bills beat the Oilers 48–17, racking up more than 500 total yards of offense for the first time in franchise history.

Buffalo's 12–2 record was easily the best in the AFL that year. The Bills hosted the Chargers, who had moved to San Diego after their first year in the league, in the AFL Championship Game. It was Kemp's chance for payback. He had led the Chargers to the 1960 and 1961 championship games. Then, in 1962, Kemp was injured. The Chargers placed him on waivers, allowing any team to sign him. The Bills did just that.

Coach Lou Saban, *left*, cheers with Pete Gogolak (3), Jack Kemp (15), and Wray Carlton (30) after the 1964 AFL Championship Game.

San Diego scored the first time it had the ball. But the Buffalo defense shut down the Chargers the rest of the way. The Bills won the AFL title with a 20–7 victory. Kemp completed 10 of 20 passes for 188 yards. Running back Cookie Gilchrist rushed for 122 yards on 16 carries. He had led the

Buffalo running back Roger Kochman tries to break through the line during a 1963 game in Houston.

AFL in rushing during the 1962 and 1964 seasons. The AFL Championship Game was his last game with the Bills.

The Bills had another strong start in 1965. They won six of their first seven games and finished 10–3–1. The AFL Championship Game was a rematch from the year before. The West champion Chargers had beaten and tied the Bills in the regular season. Buffalo's defense had allowed the fewest points in the league during the season. With Gilchrist gone and Dubenion and Bass injured, the Bills needed a strong performance from the defense.

In the AFL Championship Game, the defense outscored San Diego by itself. Butch Byrd returned an interception 74 yards for a score. Ernie Warlick scored on a touchdown pass from Kemp, and Pete Gogolak converted three field goals. Buffalo ended up winning 23–0.

"This is the only club we didn't beat this year," Saban said of the Chargers. "And, of course, we wanted this one real bad."

The Bills had won back-to-back AFL titles. But their luck was about to change for the worse.

DID YOU KNOW?

Jack Kemp, the quarterback of the Bills' 1964 and 1965 AFL championship teams, went on to a successful career in politics. He served as a US Congressman for nine terms representing western New York. He also served as secretary of Housing and Urban Development. He was the Republican Party's nominee for vice president in 1996. Kemp died in 2009 at age 73.

CHAPTER 3

MISSED
OPPORTUNITIES

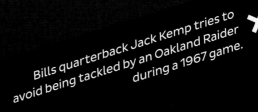

The 1966 AFL season quickly became an important one. Bills owner Ralph Wilson Jr. led the way as the AFL began working with the more established NFL. The champions of the two leagues would meet at the end of the season in the first AFL-NFL championship game. This event eventually become known as the Super Bowl.

As two-time defending AFL champions, Buffalo was a popular pick to play in the first Super Bowl. But the Bills nearly missed the playoffs. They had to win six of their last seven games to finish 9–4–1.

The AFL West champion Kansas City Chiefs came to Buffalo for the first round of the playoffs. With a win, the Bills would have a shot at their third straight AFL title.

Bills quarterback Jack Kemp tries to avoid being tackled by an Oakland Raider during a 1967 game.

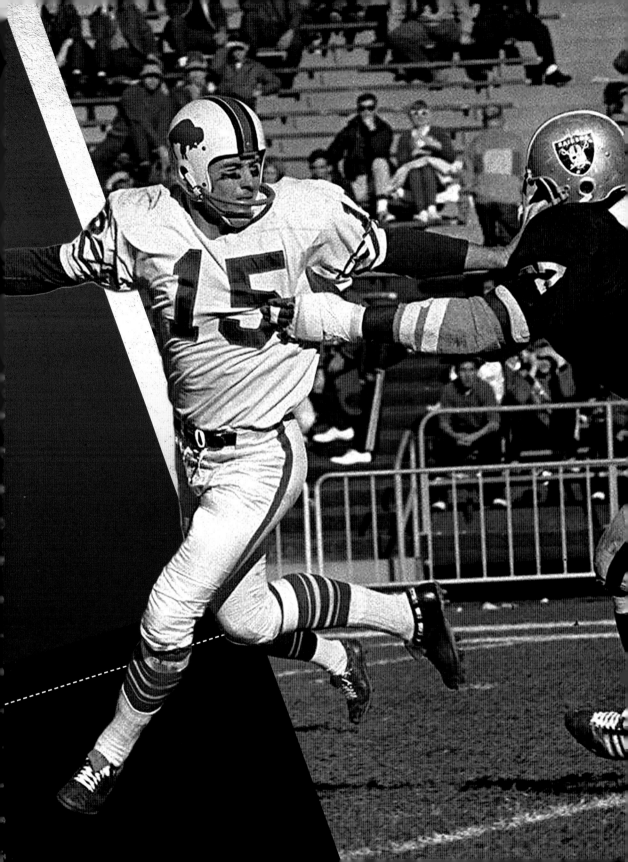

AFL ALL-TIME TEAM

The Pro Football Hall of Fame announced the AFL All-Time Team in January 1970. Three Bills were first-team selections. They were guard Billy Shaw, defensive tackle Tom Sestak, and safety George Saimes. Tackle Stew Barber, linebacker Mike Stratton, and cornerback Butch Byrd were picked for the second team. The second team also included four players who spent time with the Bills and other teams. They were running back Cookie Gilchrist, wide receiver Art Powell, defensive end Ron McDole, and defensive tackle Tom Keating.

They also would have a chance to play for a spot in the first Super Bowl.

Trouble started for the Bills when they fumbled on the opening kickoff. That set up an early Chiefs touchdown. The Bills came right back when Jack Kemp threw a 69-yard touchdown pass to Elbert Dubenion. But Buffalo did not score again. Down 14–7, the Bills reached the Kansas City 10-yard line. But Johnny Robinson intercepted a pass and returned it 72 yards. That set up a Mike Mercer field goal that gave the Chiefs a 17–7 halftime lead. Mike Garrett added two second-half touchdowns for Kansas City. The Chiefs pulled away for the 31–7 win. Buffalo had four turnovers in the game.

After those three strong seasons, the Bills began to struggle. From 1967 through 1971, Buffalo posted a combined

Bills safety Hagood Clarke (45) breaks up a pass intended for Boston Patriots receiver Jim Whalen in a 1968 game.

BILLY SHAW

Billy Shaw was the first player to spend his entire career in the AFL and be named to the Pro Football Hall of Fame. Although the Dallas Cowboys of the NFL had drafted him, Shaw decided to join the Bills in 1961. He felt like his skills would be better used in Buffalo.

After playing offense and defense at Georgia Tech, he settled in as offensive guard in Buffalo. Shaw was one of the leaders of a strong running game that gave the Bills a different look from many teams in the AFL. The league was known for its wide-open passing games. The Bills teams of the early 1960s rank as some of the top running teams in franchise history.

Shaw was a first-team AFL all-star for five consecutive seasons from 1962 to 1966. He was a second-team choice three other times. He was a member of both the All-Time AFL Team and pro football's All-Decade Team of the 1960s.

13–55–2 record. The Bills won just one game in 1968 and matched that sad feat in 1971.

While the Bills struggled on the field, they were making a transition off it. Along with nine other AFL teams, Buffalo joined the NFL in 1970. The Bills, the New York Jets, the New England Patriots, and the Miami Dolphins formed the American Football Conference (AFC) East division. The NFL's Baltimore Colts rounded out the division.

X Billy Shaw pulls out to block in a 1967 game against the Oakland Raiders. He went on to enter the Pro Football Hall of Fame.

CHAPTER 4

UPS AND DOWNS

Throughout their history, the Buffalo Bills have had extended stretches of success and disappointment. After their five-year slump at the end of the 1960s and early 1970s, the Bills began to improve. That was largely due to the return of coach Lou Saban and the emergence of running back O. J. Simpson.

Simpson ran for 1,251 yards in 1972. That was also Saban's first season back as coach. The 1972 season was the first of Simpson's five straight years of rushing for more than 1,000 yards. The Bills improved from 1–13 in 1971 to 4–9–1 in 1972. In Saban's time as a head coach, that was the only full season in which he had a losing record. But the Bills were soon back to their successful ways. They followed that season with three straight winning seasons.

O. J. Simpson looks for running room in 1973. Simpson broke the NFL single-season rushing record that year.

MILESTONE MAN

It was December 16, 1973, and O. J. Simpson had a lot to play for. The Bills were facing the New York Jets in the final game of the regular season. Simpson entered the game needing 61 yards to break Jim Brown's NFL single-season rushing record of 1,863 yards.

He took care of that feat early in the game. But there was still more work to be done. A week earlier, Simpson had rushed for 219 yards in a win over New England, his second 200-yard game that season. No NFL running back had ever rushed for 200 yards in consecutive games or in three games in the same season. Simpson was determined to break a few more records that day.

Simpson's final carry against the Jets was a 7-yard run that left him with 200 yards on the nose. It also pushed his season total to 2,003 rushing yards, making him the first NFL player to rush for more than 2,000 yards in a season. Simpson's teammates carried him off the field on their shoulders to celebrate his historic effort.

Rookie Joe Ferguson took over as quarterback in 1973. It was the first of his 12 straight seasons as the Bills' starter. The emphasis in Buffalo, however, remained on the running game. Simpson became the first 2,000-yard rusher in NFL history with 2,003 yards that season. He led the Bills to a season-ending four-game winning streak and a 9–5 record.

Simpson's rushing numbers dropped steeply in 1974. But Ferguson's passing production was on the rise. The Bills started the season 7–1, enough to get them headed toward the playoffs. By the time they arrived at the postseason with a 9–5 record, however, they were struggling. The Pittsburgh Steelers ruined Buffalo's first playoff appearance in eight years. It was also Buffalo's first playoff appearance as a member of the NFL. Pittsburgh's "Steel Curtain" defense held Simpson to 49 rushing yards in the 32–14 loss.

Buffalo's offense peaked during the 1975 season. Simpson rushed for 1,817 yards, while Ferguson improved his production to 2,426 passing yards and an NFL-best 25 touchdown passes. As a result, the Bills led the league in scoring with an average of 30 points per game. That would not be enough, though. The Bills started the season with four straight wins, but they fell short of the playoffs with a disappointing 8–6 finish.

2,000-YARD CLUB

Buffalo's O. J. Simpson was the only player to rush for 2,000 yards in a 14-game NFL season. He rushed 332 times for 2,003 yards and 12 touchdowns in 1973. Six players have run for more than 2,000 yards in a 16-game NFL season. Eric Dickerson ran for a record 2,105 yards for the Los Angeles Rams in 1984. Detroit's Barry Sanders ran for 2,053 in 1997. Then, Denver's Terrell Davis ran for 2,008 the next year. Jamal Lewis of the Baltimore Ravens gained 2,066 in 2003. Tennessee's Chris Johnson rushed for 2,006 in 2009, and Minnesota's Adrian Peterson posted 2,097 rushing yards in 2012.

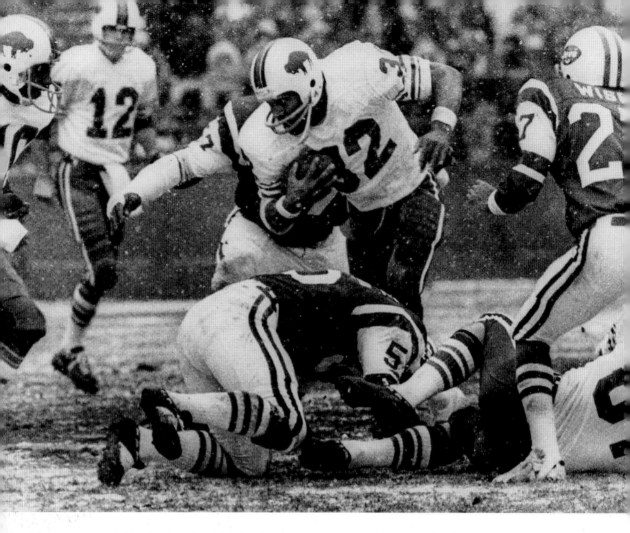

✕ O. J. Simpson bursts through the New York Jets' defensive line to set the NFL season rushing record in 1973.

Saban left the team after a 2–3 start in 1976. He quit when team management stripped him of some of his responsibilities. The players seemed to miss him. Under new coach Jim Ringo, the Bills lost the rest of their games to finish 2–12.

Buffalo's ups and downs continued. Ringo lost his job after going 3–11 in 1977. The Bills turned to Chuck Knox, who had led the Los Angeles Rams to five straight division titles. It took Knox a couple of years to right the ship in Buffalo, but he led the Bills to playoff berths in 1980 and 1981.

The 1980 team finished 11–5. The offense was led by all-purpose running back Joe Cribbs. He ran for 1,185 yards and caught 52 passes for another 415 yards. Meanwhile, the Bills' defense allowed the fewest yards in the league. They won the AFC East title, but as one of five 11–5 teams in the conference that season, the Bills lost a tiebreaker and had to open the

ELECTRIC COMPANY

A good running back usually runs behind a good offensive line. O. J. Simpson was no exception. Joe DeLamielleure and Reggie McKenzie led the Bills' offensive line during Simpson's time in Buffalo. Simpson was nicknamed "Juice." The line earned a nickname of its own: "Electric Company." That was because it "turned the Juice loose." *Juice* was a slang term for electricity.

DeLamielleure was a first- or second-team All-Pro eight times. After playing seven seasons with the Bills, he spent five years in Cleveland. He completed his career with one more year in Buffalo. He was selected to the NFL's All-Decade Team for the 1970s. In 2003 he was inducted into the Pro Football Hall of Fame.

McKenzie was first-team All-Pro in 1973, Simpson's 2,000-yard season. McKenzie was second-team All-Pro the following two seasons.

playoffs on the road at San Diego. Buffalo led 14–3 at halftime. But Ferguson threw three interceptions for the Bills, and Chargers quarterback Dan Fouts led a second-half comeback. His 50-yard touchdown pass to receiver Ron Smith with just over two minutes to play gave San Diego the 20–14 win.

In 1981 Ferguson passed for a career-high 3,652 yards. Cribbs also topped 1,000 rushing yards that year, while Frank Lewis had 1,244 receiving yards. A late surge helped the Bills finish 10–6 and claim a wild-card berth. The Bills took a 24–0 lead against the Jets in their first playoff game and held on to win 31–27. Lewis caught seven passes for 158 yards, including two touchdowns. The next week in Cincinnati, Bengals quarterback Ken Anderson hit wide receiver Cris Collinsworth with a 16-yard touchdown pass early in the fourth quarter to lift Cincinnati over the Bills 28–21.

TARNISHED IMAGE

O. J. Simpson had been a record-setting running back and later a popular sports broadcaster and actor. But in 1994, everything changed. Simpson was charged with the murder of his former wife and her friend. After a controversial, high-profile trial, he was found not guilty in 1995. But in 2008, following an incident in a Las Vegas hotel room, Simpson was found guilty of armed robbery, kidnapping, and other charges. He was originally sentenced to 33 years in prison, but he was released in 2017.

✗ Quarterback Jim Kelly helped turn the Bills into Super Bowl contenders soon after joining the team in 1986.

The Bills fell short of the playoffs the next six years, a streak that included back-to-back 2–14 seasons in 1984 and 1985. But the arrival of quarterback Jim Kelly and head coach Marv Levy in 1986 set the stage for the most successful period in Buffalo football history.

CHAPTER 5

SUSTAINED EXCELLENCE

Four future Hall of Famers in the primes of their careers starred for the Bills in the early 1990s. Those players were key in helping Buffalo reach the Super Bowl for four straight seasons. They were quarterback Jim Kelly, running back Thurman Thomas, wide receiver Andre Reed, and defensive end Bruce Smith. Behind that talented quartet, the Bills made the playoffs 10 times between 1988 and 1999.

After six seasons without a winning record, the Bills started 11–1 in 1988, ending up at 12–4. In their first playoff game, the defense forced three turnovers in a 17–10 defeat of the Houston Oilers. Their luck ran out, however, in another fruitless trip to Cincinnati. This time, Kelly threw

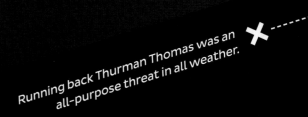

Running back Thurman Thomas was an all-purpose threat in all weather.

THURMAN THOMAS

His elite pass-catching and running abilities made Thurman Thomas a big part of the Bills' high-powered no-huddle offense. He led the league in total offense for four straight seasons. When he retired, Thomas ranked ninth in the NFL in rushing with 12,074 yards. He added another 4,458 yards on 472 receptions. Thomas scored 88 touchdowns in his 13-year career. The former Oklahoma State All-American was inducted into the Pro Football Hall of Fame in 2007.

three interceptions as the Bengals pulled out a 21–10 win in the AFC Championship Game.

Kelly, Thomas, and Reed led an explosive offense that helped the Bills win the division again in 1989. The defense was not as strong that year, however. Against the Cleveland Browns in the playoffs, Kelly passed for 405 yards and four touchdowns. But the Bills still lost, 34–30.

After the loss to the Browns, the Bills won 10 straight AFC playoff games. Those led to the four straight Super Bowl appearances. However, the Bills missed the playoffs following the 1994 season. When they returned to the playoffs after the 1995 season, they lost 40–21 to the Pittsburgh Steelers in a divisional playoff game to end the streak.

Thomas had the last of his 1,000-yard rushing seasons in 1996. The aging Bills still had enough gas in the tank to win

10 games and a wild-card berth that season. They even held a late lead in the playoffs against Jacksonville after Jeff Burris returned an interception 38 yards for a touchdown early in the fourth quarter. But the Jaguars scored the final 10 points of the game and pulled out the victory 30–27.

Kelly retired after the 1996 season. A year later, Smith posted the last of his eight first-team All-Pro seasons. Reed ended a 10-year stretch in which he led the team in receiving nine times. The faces in Buffalo were beginning to change.

With Doug Flutie at quarterback, Buffalo got back to the playoffs after the 1998 and 1999 seasons. But the Bills suffered two painful losses. In 1998 the Bills played the Miami Dolphins in the wild-card round of the playoffs. Flutie passed for 360 yards in the game. Wide receiver Eric Moulds caught nine passes for 240 yards. But the Bills lost 24–17.

BY THE NUMBERS

From 1990 to 1995, the Bills won 10 straight AFC playoff games. Their most frequent opponent in that stretch was the Miami Dolphins, whom they faced in 1990, 1992, and 1995. The biggest win was a 51–3 victory over the Los Angeles Raiders in January 1991. The Bills' closest game was a three-point win, which happened twice. In January 1992, the Bills beat the Denver Broncos 10–7. In January 1993, the Bills beat the Houston Oilers 41–38 in overtime after trailing 35–3. The Bills outscored their opponents 332–167 in those 10 victories.

✕ Defensive end Bruce Smith celebrates one of his many big plays for the Bills.

The 1999 Bills won seven of their final nine games to reach the playoffs again. They played the Tennessee Titans. In his last game with the team, Smith had 2.5 sacks. The Bills appeared to have won the game. But then "the Music City Miracle" broke

BRUCE SMITH

Defensive end Bruce Smith set an NFL record with 200 quarterback sacks. He made the NFL's All-Decade Team for both the 1980s and 1990s. Smith's speed and moves made him almost impossible to stop. Opponents frequently double-teamed and even triple-teamed him in an attempt to keep him from disrupting their offenses.

Smith played for the Bills from 1985 to 1999 and Washington from 2000 to 2003. The All-American from Virginia Tech lived up to expectations as the first player selected in the 1985 NFL Draft. He was named AFC Defensive Rookie of the Year before twice being named NFL Defensive Player of the Year. He was honored a total of four times as the top defensive player in the AFC. Smith also gave the Bills a 12–3 lead in Super Bowl XXV. He sacked New York Giants quarterback Jeff Hostetler in the end zone for a safety. Smith was inducted into the Pro Football Hall of Fame in 2009.

the hearts of Buffalo fans. Steve Christie's 41-yard field goal gave Buffalo a 16–15 lead with just seconds remaining. But on the ensuing kickoff, the Titans' Kevin Dyson took a lateral 75 yards for the winning score. One of the most famous plays in NFL history gave Tennessee a 22–16 victory.

That loss was the last time Buffalo would see the playoffs for almost 20 years. The Bills struggled throughout the 2000s with an erratic group of quarterbacks that included, among others, Drew Bledsoe, J. P. Losman, and Ryan Fitzpatrick.

The team seemed to change coaches or quarterbacks nearly every season. It left Buffalo fans frustrated as the Bills were consistently left out of the AFC playoff picture.

Buffalo went 17 seasons without playing in the postseason. That was the most of any team in the NFL, the National Basketball Association, Major League Baseball, or the National Hockey League. The streak finally ended in 2017. On December 31, the Bills defeated the Dolphins to finish 9–7. Buffalo then needed the Bengals to beat the Ravens to get into the playoffs. In the final minute, Bengals quarterback Andy Dalton threw a 49-yard touchdown pass to give Cincinnati the win and knock Baltimore out of the playoff race. The Bills had reached the postseason for the first time since 1999.

Buffalo didn't make it past the first round, losing a gritty defensive struggle 10–3 at Jacksonville. But thanks in part to first-year head coach Sean McDermott, the Bills appeared to have a promising future ahead of them.

In 2018 Buffalo selected quarterback Josh Allen from the University of Wyoming in the first round of the NFL Draft. Allen went through the typical ups and downs of a rookie, but he proved to be a threat with his arm and his feet even though the team's record slipped to 6–10.

✕ Defensive end Jerry Hughes lines up to rush the quarterback in the 2017 AFC playoffs.

Allen rushed for 631 yards and eight touchdowns in just 11 starts. He even made history in December, becoming the first quarterback since the AFL-NFL merger to rush for more than 100 yards in consecutive games. It was enough to give Bills fans hope that the team had finally found a franchise quarterback who could lead a return to regular playoff berths in Buffalo.

TIMELINE

The Buffalo Bills and Boston Patriots join six charter members preparing for the first season of the American Football League.

✗ **1959**

Buffalo loses its first game 27–3 to the New York Titans.

✗ **1960**

The Bills beat the San Diego Chargers 20–7 in the AFL Championship Game.

✗ **1964**

The Bills shut out the Chargers 23–0 to repeat as AFL champions.

✗ **1965**

Buffalo loses to Kansas City 31–7 in the AFL Championship Game on January 1, missing a chance to play in the first Super Bowl.

✗ **1967**

The Bills and nine other AFL franchises merge into the NFL.

✗ **1970**

Bills running back O. J. Simpson becomes the first in NFL history to rush for more than 2,000 yards in a season.

✗ **1973**

Marv Levy takes over as head coach.

✗ **1986**

The Bills start a streak of 10 straight wins in AFC playoff games.

✗ **1990**

The New York Giants edge Buffalo 20–19 on January 27 in Super Bowl XXV.

✗ **1991**

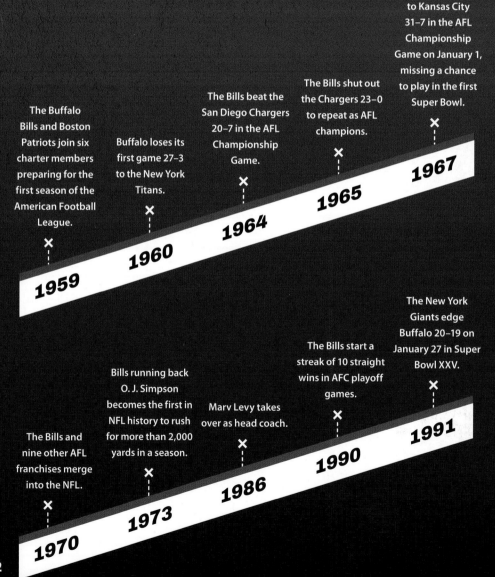

Washington beats the Bills 37–24 on January 26 in Super Bowl XXVI.

✕

The Bills produce the biggest comeback in NFL playoff history on January 3, rallying from 35–3 to defeat the Houston Oilers 41–38 in overtime.

✕

The Dallas Cowboys pound the Bills 52–17 on January 31 in Super Bowl XXVII.

✕

Dallas beats Buffalo 30–13 on January 30 in Super Bowl XXVIII.

✕

The Bills win the last of their 10 straight AFC playoff games 37–22 over the Miami Dolphins on December 30.

✕

1992

1993

1993

1994

1995

Buffalo qualifies for the playoffs for the tenth time in 12 years.

✕

"The Music City Miracle," a 75-yard kickoff return with the help of a lateral, allows Tennessee to pull out a 22–16 playoff victory over the Bills on January 8.

✕

The Bills begin a streak of 17 years without a playoff appearance.

✕

Rookie head coach Sean McDermott leads the Bills to the playoffs for the first time in 17 years, but they lose in the first round to Jacksonville.

✕

First-year quarterback Josh Allen rushes for 631 yards and eight touchdowns, but the Bills finish 6–10.

✕

1999

2000

2000

2017

2018

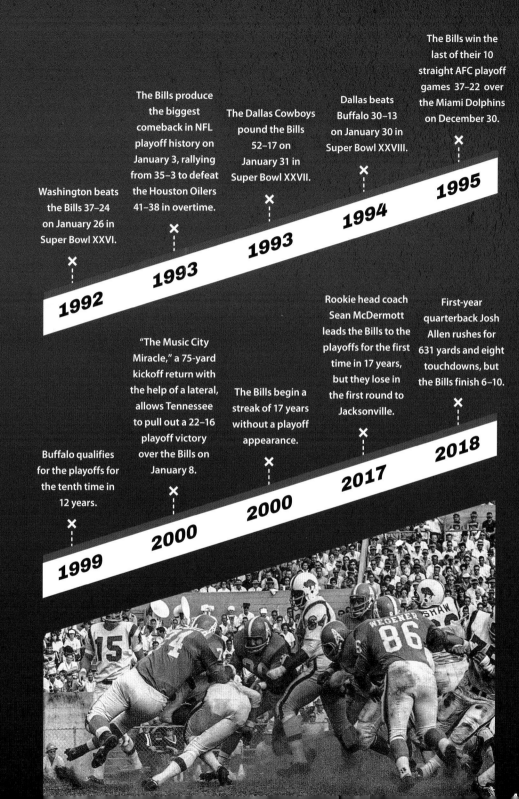

QUICK STATS

FRANCHISE HISTORY

1960–69 (AFL)
1970– (NFL)

SUPER BOWLS
(wins in bold)

1990 (XXV), 1991 (XXVI),
1992 (XXVII), 1993 (XXVIII)

AFL CHAMPIONSHIP GAMES *(1960–69, wins in bold)*

1964, **1965**, 1966

AFC CHAMPIONSHIP GAMES *(since 1970 AFL-NFL merger)*

1988, 1990, 1991, 1992, 1993

DIVISION CHAMPIONSHIPS *(since 1970 AFL-NFL merger)*

1980, 1988, 1989, 1990, 1991,
1993, 1995

KEY PLAYERS
(position, seasons with team)

Joe DeLamielleure
(G, 1973–79, 1985)
Joe Ferguson (QB, 1973–84)
Jim Kelly (QB, 1986–96)
Jack Kemp (QB, 1962–69)
Reggie McKenzie (G, 1972–82)
Eric Moulds (WR, 1996–2005)
Andre Reed (WR, 1985–99)
Billy Shaw (G, 1961–69)
O. J. Simpson (RB, 1969–77)
Bruce Smith (DE, 1985–99)
Thurman Thomas (RB, 1988–99)

KEY COACHES

Marv Levy (1986–97): 112–70,
11–8 (playoffs)
Lou Saban (1962–65, 1972–76):
68–45–4, 2–2 (playoffs)

HOME FIELDS

New Era Field (1973–)
Also known as Rich Stadium,
Ralph Wilson Stadium
War Memorial Stadium (1960–72)

*All statistics through 2018 season

QUOTES AND ANECDOTES

Buffalo Bills running back Thurman Thomas missed the opening possession of Super Bowl XXVI when he misplaced his helmet. It was a bad omen for the Bills, who went on to lose to Washington 37–24.

Linebacker Mike Stratton was one of the defensive leaders when the Bills won their two AFL championships. Had the Super Bowl been created two years earlier, Buffalo would have faced off against the NFL champion Cleveland Browns in 1964. They would have faced the NFL champion Green Bay Packers in 1965. Had that been the case, Stratton believed Buffalo would have won a Super Bowl. "I would have relished the opportunity," Stratton told *USA Today* in 2009. "And, I would have picked us."

During his lengthy career in sports, Lou Saban also served as president of the New York Yankees baseball team. "He has been my friend and mentor for over 50 years, and one of the people who helped shape my life," said former Yankees owner George Steinbrenner. He brought Saban to the Yankees for the 1981 and 1982 seasons. Steinbrenner had coached wide receivers on Saban's staff at Northwestern University in 1955. Saban died in 2009. He was 87.

For many years in the late 2000s, Buffalo fans were worried their team was moving to Toronto. The team was regularly playing games in Canada. Millionaires in Canada were looking into buying the team and moving it north. But Terry Pegula stepped forward and bought the team. The Bills continue to call Buffalo home.

GLOSSARY

comeback
When a team losing a game rallies to tie the score or take the lead.

contender
A person or team that has a good chance at winning a championship.

draft
A system that allows teams to acquire new players coming into a league.

franchise
A sports organization, including the top-level team and all minor league affiliates.

hall of fame
A place built to honor noteworthy achievements by athletes in their respective sports.

lateral
A pass that goes sideways or backward.

merge
Join with another to create something new, such as a company, a team, or a league.

retire
To end one's career.

rookie
A professional athlete in his or her first year of competition.

waivers
The process of making a player available to other teams in the league.

wild card
A team that makes the playoffs even though it did not win its division.

MORE
INFORMATION

BOOKS

Cohn, Nate. *Buffalo Bills*. New York: AV2 by Weigl, 2018.

Kortemeier, Todd. *Buffalo Bills*. Minneapolis, MN: Abdo Publishing, 2017.

Scheff, Matt. *The Best NFL Running Backs of All Time*. Minneapolis, MN: Abdo Publishing, 2013.

ONLINE RESOURCES

To learn more about the Buffalo Bills, visit **abdobooklinks.com** or scan this QR code. These links are routinely monitored and updated to provide the most current information available.

PLACE TO VISIT

Pro Football Hall of Fame
2121 George Halas Drive NW
Canton, OH 44708
330–456–8207
profootballhof.com

This hall of fame and museum highlights the greatest players and moments in the history of the AFL and the NFL. People affiliated with the Buffalo Bills who are enshrined there include Andre Reed, Jim Kelly, and former owner Ralph Wilson Jr.

INDEX

ABOUT THE AUTHOR

Tony Hunter is a writer from Castle Rock, Colorado. This is his first children's book series. He lives with his daughter and his trusty Rottweiler, Dan.